FALL GUYS

THE UNOFFICIAL GUIDE TO STAYING ON TOP

STÉPHANE PILET

Andrews McMeel
PUBLISHING®

Published in French under the title *Fall Guys: le guide de jeu* © 2021 404 éditions, an imprint of Édi8, Paris, France

Andrews McMeel Publishing
a division of Andrews McMeel Universal
1130 Walnut Street, Kansas City, Missouri 64106

www.andrewsmcmeel.com

21 22 23 24 25 RR2 10 9 8 7 6 5 4 3 2 1

ISBN: 978-1-5248-6836-9

Library of Congress Control Number: 2021931289

Made by:
LSC Communications US, LLC
Address and location of manufacturer:
1009 Sloan Street
Crawfordsville, IN 47933
1st Printing—3/8/21

ATTENTION: SCHOOLS AND BUSINESSES
Andrews McMeel books are available at quantity discounts with bulk purchase for educational, business, or sales promotional use. For information, please e-mail the Andrews McMeel Publishing Special Sales Department: specialsales@amuniversal.com.

INTRODUCTION

In a matter of weeks, the awkward and adorable jellybean characters of *Fall Guys: Ultimate Knockout* won the hearts of gamers worldwide. *Fall Guys* has really simple controls, varied rounds that use all your skills, and it's a blast to play with friends!

But *Fall Guys* is also a game full of complexities! And this guide can help you figure them out and win the crown. You'll learn how to stay on your feet and discover the best tips to master each round and qualify all the way through.

Fall Guys is a constantly evolving game. The types of rounds can change, and new ones appear regularly. This book was completed in season 3, so don't be surprised if newer rounds aren't included.

Happy reading!

Stef Leflou

Cool Beans

The lovable beans of *Fall Guys* have been Twitch and YouTube superstars for some time now, but here's what you need to know if you're new to their world.

In *Fall Guys*, you have sixty beans competing against one another in five rounds, each wackier than the last. The goal is to get first place and become master of the beans, but you have to qualify in each round to move on to the next. The number of qualified players in each round depends both on the round and the number of players. Players are eliminated in every round until only one player remains. Here are the main types of rounds in *Fall Guys*.

RACE

There are many race rounds, and they are all very different. You won't get eliminated if you fall off the course into the void, but you will get eliminated if you fail to cross the finish line before the round reaches its number of qualified players. (That number is displayed at the top right of your screen.)

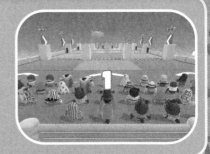

SURVIVAL

The survival rounds are not forgiving. If you fall, you get eliminated. In some rounds, you have to stay alive until there are only a certain number of beans left. Sometimes, accidents happen and there will be fewer beans who qualify than expected. That's a good thing. It means you'll have fewer opponents in the final.

(It could even mean the final round will happen sooner than expected.)

TEAM

Team rounds can be really bad for beans that already find solo rounds stressful. Depending on when they happen (and therefore the number of participants), you can have two, three, or four teams competing. The more players there are, the harder the round—coordinating a big team isn't always easy. If you play with friends, you'll all be together during the team events, which will give you an advantage. As you've probably guessed, the players on the team with the lowest score are eliminated.

FINAL

Whatever the final round ends up being, there will only be one bean left standing. In these rounds, like the others, anything goes. The winner gets a shiny crown that they can then spend in the store to become the most stylish bean in town.

WHY DO BEANS FALL?

As a bean, you already know this: you fall often! This chapter will help you understand why. You'll find advice that can help you avoid potentially fatal falls ... Well ... let's hope!

1 THEY TRIP

Beans tend to trip very easily. They can't help it. With their round body, short legs, and small feet, they're not built for balance. When your bean stumbles, it'll lean a bit to try to regain its balance. If you jump at this point or if you speed up (by going down a slope, for example), you'll surely fall. When you trip, try to stay on a level surface, slow down, and most importantly, don't jump!

2 THEY FALL FROM HIGH UP

Most beans that fall from a significant height will not land on their feet. If a bean utters a little cry ("Woooo") during a fall, it means they've fallen from too high up. When that happens, it'll roll on the ground when it lands, costing you precious time in a race. (But don't worry—they don't get hurt when they fall.) If you're falling from high up, try to dive before you hit the ground. You'll lose less time that way.

③ THEY LAND ON PLATFORM EDGES

You have to be careful when you jump on a platform. If you land on an edge, you'll fall. When you jump, try to make sure you're not going to land on an edge.

④ THEY LAND ON OTHER BEANS

At the start of rounds, beans are often very close together. And you've probably noticed a lot of them falling in the initial chaos. That's because you'll fall if you jump and land on a bean in front of you. To avoid this, try not to jump when you're in a crowd of beans.

5 THEY GO TOO FAST

To win, you have to be faster than other beans. But when beans go too fast, they can trip and fall—especially if they're jumping. Be careful in races with sloping ramps and conveyor belts: these can increase your speed. Depending on the situation, you can dive when you notice you're tripping or just slow down a bit to regain your balance.

6 THEIR FEET GET CAUGHT ON EDGES

You may have noticed edges in between platforms in some rounds. These don't usually make you fall if you're walking normally. But if you jump just as you're going over one, you might not make it. In rounds like Jump Club, that means you could get eliminated if you mess up a jump when you're trying to get over the beam. When this happens, you can see a small white cloud at your feet, similar to the one you see when you land after a jump.

HOW TO AVOID FALLING AFTER A JUMP

Beans usually fall after a jump when they're not perpendicular to an obstacle. Many platforms are slightly rounded or sloping, which increases your risk of falling. To counter this, try to be as perpendicular as you can to the edge of the platform you're jumping on or off. This way, when you land, both of your feet should touch the ground at the same time.

(Don't) Catch Them All!

Before coming to blows with another bean, make sure you can defend yourself! Often, a bean that's been grabbed will get angry and try to knock you down. Here's what you need to remember if someone's looking for a fight.

1 PUSH AN OPPONENT

When you grab a player with your little arms, you can hold them for a second. After that, you'll push them back. Be careful: this will also push you backward a bit, so avoid grabbing another bean if you are at the edge of a platform. Otherwise you could be the one who falls. (And the other beans will laugh at you!)

2 PUSHING AS A TEAM

If two beans grab a third bean and they're facing the same direction, the target bean will be pushed twice as far. This can be very handy to remember during survival events, where falling off a platform can eliminate players. If you get pushed off, it's probably because two players grabbed you at the same time!

3 TEMPORARY PROTECTION

When a bean is grabbed and pushed by another bean, it can't be grabbed by anyone else for one second. This is a good thing. If it weren't the case, it would let mean players gang up on one bean.

4 USE THE SLIME

If you grab a player and you are on a slimy surface (like in Slime Climb), when you let them go, they'll be pushed much farther than usual thanks to all that slippery goo. If the pushed player is on a slope, it can be even funnier to watch! If this happens to you, dive forward to limit the damage.

5 NEGATE A GRAB

When a bean grabs you, you have a second to react and grab it back (after which you'll be pushed). When this happens, you'll be holding one another by the arms. And as long as you both hold the grab button, you can't shove one another. Whoever lets go first will be pushed.

6 THE BEAN DANCE

When two players cling to one another, it's harder to move. If one player pushes in one direction and the other doesn't move, it will slowly move them anyway. If both players try to move forward, they'll stay still. There is only one exception: if the players are on a slope, the one facing downhill has gravity on their side and can push the other bean.

7 CRAB WALK

If you and another player are grabbing each other and neither wants to let go, try walking sideways. Just like when you push a player, you'll move more slowly. Moving sideways will allow you to move an opponent to a dangerous platform or get yourself out of a potentially messy situation.

8 QUICK GRAB

If you grab a bean for less than a second, it won't be thrown back, but it will give you more stability. This can be useful in rounds like Perfect Match, Roll Out, or other survival rounds where falling can eliminate you.

9 SNEAK ATTACK

Sometimes you can come across a bean who's not paying attention. You can take this opportunity to grab them from behind and push them. If they're not facing you, they can't grab you back—so take advantage of it! Sometimes you've got to be a ruthless bean to win. This tip also works if you're grabbing a bean from the side.

10 SLOW AN OPPONENT DOWN

In team rounds, grabbing an opponent is a good way to prevent them from playing properly. In Egg Scramble, you have to make opponents drop their eggs. In the rounds with balls, you can grab other players to prevent them from hitting the ball or getting too close to it.

11 PULLING THEIR SHIRT

This trick consists of catching a player and then releasing them immediately. There are two pluses to doing this. First, the player who is grabbed and released moves back just slightly, which can sometimes allow you to pass them. But the best part about doing this is that the other bean can't jump for a quarter of a second after. Grabbing a player just before a jump can knock them down. And in addition to being extremely funny, it can help you win Jump Showdown or Hex-A-Gone (if you remember to jump immediately after you pull their shirt).

12 FALL ON PURPOSE

There are rounds where it can help you to fall on purpose, such as Tail Tag. When you fall and roll on the ground, the other beans can't grab you and no one can steal your tail. To fall, all you have to do is jump on a platform edge or deliberately get hit by a rotating hammer.

13 CATCH WHILE JUMPING

This technique is mainly used in Tail Tag, Team Tail Tag, and Royal Fumble. It can even land you a qualification if, at the end of the event, you still don't have a tail. You have to use the jump button first, then dive forward by pressing the button to grab an opponent. This also allows you to dive farther.

SEE SAW

ROUND TYPE
RACE

This round will make you hate other beans. You have to run across a series of platforms that all tilt dangerously when too many players gather on the same side. You've got to tilt them just right!

1 THE START

Your position at the start of the round will have a big impact on how you'll place. If you start at the front of the pack, you'll have an advantage, since there will be fewer players tilting the seesaws. If you start in the second, third, or fourth row, it'll be a bit harder. If you start farther back, try to go to the seesaws with the fewest beans. Crowds are your worst enemy in this round.

2 STAY IN THE MIDDLE

Go to the middle of the seesaws when you can so you don't tilt them too much. When you can't, go to the side with the fewest players. This will prevent the platform from tilting too quickly and can help keep you from falling.

3 WHEN TO DIVE

Diving to get to the next platform can be very useful. It can also help you gain stability if the seesaw starts to tilt too far. When that happens, dive while aiming for the middle of the platform or for the higher side so that your weight helps to stabilize it. You can also dive after a jump to help you avoid tripping and rolling.

4 THE BARRIERS

Between each platform, there are checkpoints. You can use these so you don't have to start the course over from the beginning. You can also jump up on the barriers and use them to reach the next platform. They can lead you to the center of the seesaws and help you avoid accidents. Just be careful not to fall off!

5 THE YEETUS

Sometimes a large spinning hammer, otherwise known as a big yeetus, appears near the end of the course. Avoid it if you can. If you can't, try to plan around it and jump when the hammer is down. That way, when it hits, it will propel you as high as possible. It's a good idea to dive when you're about to land to soften your landing.

6 SEESAW POSITION

Occasionally, some platforms (near the end of the course) are positioned to tilt in the direction of the course. You can always wait a bit for other players to arrive and raise the platform to help you reach the checkpoint safely.

GATE CRASH

This round will test your ability to plan ahead. You'll have to go through a series of moving doors that slide open and closed vertically, temporarily restricting access to the rest of the course. Be careful—some doors take longer than others to open.

1 PLAN

Head toward the doors that are blocking your way. By the time you get to them, they should be low enough so you can keep running.

2 JUMP

If you get to a door right as it's starting to rise again, jump to avoid tripping on it or getting stuck on the wrong side. It's better if you can get through without having to jump so you don't slow down. Be careful to not land on another player if you jump. This will make you fall and slow you down.

3 DIVE

When a door is rising, you can try to jump and dive right after so you don't get stuck. You can get to the other side even if your feet touch the door, so it's worth giving it a shot.

4 NARROW DOORS

Near the end of the course, you'll have to go through slightly narrower doors. Be careful—the ones on the sides stay closed longer than those in the middle. Watch out for the moving donut bumpers as well. (You can dive to avoid them if you need to.) If there's a crowd of players, try to stay near the middle of the door so you're not pushed off to the side. When a bunch of beans crowd together into a small space, it can get ugly!

5 FINAL JUMP

The last part of the course before the finish line has a steep slope coated in slime and a ditch just before the final doors. When you make your way down that slope, aim for the door that is rising. That way, you'll be in front of the ditch as it opens. Depending on how high the door is, all you might need is a simple jump. But diving will help you make it to the finish line faster.

HIT PARADE

This round will require a number of skills: planning, diving, camera movement, and control in the last part of the race.

1 LET IT GO

Rather than balancing on the beams, you can drop right to the platform below. Just start between two beams as pictured to make sure you don't land on an obstacle below. Slow down a bit before you drop. That way you don't have to roll when you land, and you'll gain some speed on your way down. Slow down a bit before reaching the slope so you don't fall. Doing this should bring you to the head of the pack.

2 THE REVOLVING DOORS

Depending on the game, you either have to go through turnstiles or rotating beams (just like in Jump Club, but smaller). If you're facing the turnstiles, follow the other beans. The combined strength of the group will make them move. Plan your moves before you get to the sliding wall. It usually works out better when you approach it from the side, so you don't get jostled by the crowd going through the center.

3 THE BEAMS

To make it through the rotating beams, go between the two circles on the ground. That way, you only have to jump once to get past them. If you dropped at the beginning of the course and you're already in the lead, this tactic will help you widen the gap, potentially letting you finish first!

4 THE PENDULUMS

Each giant pendulum that swings across the course path can knock you off the side. Sometimes they swing in the same direction as the course, making them a bit less dangerous. Use your camera to help gauge the distance between you and these pendulums. You can also travel along the edges of the course. But be careful: the slightest thing could make you fall!

5 THE SLIME CLIMB

The last part of this course can be tough. In some games, you'll have to avoid moving donut bumpers or rotating hammers. The hill is covered in slime so it's easy to slip. Getting hit can slow you down or push you backward, so plan your moves carefully. Hammers and bumpers can propel you forward if they hit you from behind.

6 ALTERNATE VERSIONS

Just before the final climb, sometimes there are huge, thicc bonkuses instead of pendulums. Plan your moves to get through without getting crushed—or worse—knocked off the side.

DIZZY HEIGHTS

ROUND TYPE
RACE

This round will make your head spin. Here's what you need to remember to get through each part of the course while keeping your cool.

1 WHICH WAY?

Pay close attention to the way the plates are spinning. You want to choose them strategically. Decide where you want to end up, and pick the plates that will move you in that direction. That way you're not fighting against them, and you can maintain a constant speed.

2 JUMP OR NOT?

It's a good idea to avoid jumping on the spinning plates in the first part of the course. That's for two reasons: you could land on another player and fall, and jumping will slow you down. Remember, you don't need to jump to get through this part of the course.

3 BE AGILE

Here you have to avoid big balls that cannons shoot regularly into each lane. Try not to hit the walls and get slowed down, and try to change lanes as soon as you see the cannon getting ready to shoot a ball. If you don't manage to change lanes in time, dive before a ball hits you so you don't get pushed back too far. You can avoid changing lanes if the ball comes when you're in an intersection. Then you can move just slightly to the right, as if you were going to change lanes. When the ball has passed, you can return to the lane you were in and keep going. That way, you don't have to worry about another ball immediately.

4 IT'S JUMP O'CLOCK

You're going to come across some more spinning plates. If you can, go to the right. That direction will give you a more direct route than going to the left. You don't have to dive here, unless you need to compensate for a short jump and you're about to fall. Watch out: sometimes there are swinging pendulums and sometimes there are thicc bonkuses above the spinning plates. Take care or they'll knock you over!

5 IF YOU FALL

If you fall off the spinning plates, you land in a passage that has rotating walls with holes them. You have to jump to get through each wall. Don't worry if you fall. You won't be eliminated—you'll just lose a little time. You can still qualify by catching up in the last part of the course.

6 THEY'RE GONE!

Sometimes there aren't any spinning plates. If this happens, jump to the section in the middle. It's pretty likely that you'll fall and end up in that passage with the rotating walls. No matter what, try to avoid bouncing too high. It'll just slow you down.

7 SWAN DIVE

To reach the finish line, you have to make a particularly dangerous leap. You can make it by jumping and then diving to ensure you land on the spinning plates. But you can also jump at the last moment and not waste any time landing.

8 GET A BOOST

If the yeetus appears in the middle, you can use it to propel yourself straight to the finish line. Approach it from either side and place yourself in front of it when the hammer is raised. Be sure to jump before you get hit so you get propelled even farther.

9 DODGE THE BALLS

Let the movement of the spinning platform propel your jump to the next one. If you see a ball heading your way and you don't have time to avoid it, dive so you don't get pushed back. You just have to reach the finish line and avoid the balls. (For whatever reason, sometimes the balls are replaced by fruit.) At this point, you're likely to qualify.

10 ALTERNATE VERSIONS

Sometimes the large spinning plates at the end are replaced by smaller spinning plates or fixed circular platforms with rotating beams that can knock you down.

DOOR DASH

ROUND TYPE
RACE

In this round, you have to go through a series of doors to get to the finish line. It's easy—except that the course narrows after each door . . . and most of them are actually walls you can't go through!

1 TRUE OR FALSE

It's hard to tell a real door from a fake one. Look at the small white triangle in the bottom middle of each door. When the triangle is smaller than the others, it's a real door you can go through.

2 PAY ATTENTION

At the beginning, you'll notice the seven walls in the course. Pay attention—especially to the last three doors. You can only get through one of them. It seems like the true door is slightly smaller and narrower than the others.

3 JUMP CAREFULLY

As you progress through the course, there are fewer and fewer doors you can go through. This makes it tricky to jump because you're crowded together. If you see a crowd in front of a door, try to dive after you jump to make sure you get through.

4 THE FINAL JUMP

When you go through the last door, try to avoid diving until the last possible moment before you land. That way you'll spend less time getting up. If there's a yeetus, you can use it to propel yourself to the front of the group.

TIP TOE

For this round, you'll need to maintain your self-control and stay on your toes. To reach the finish line, you have to use the tiles that light up. If you use any others, you'll fall through!

1 THE START

You can go for it at the beginning by jumping and diving to quickly find which tiles on the course will let you get to the finish line. Pay close attention: the tiles will only light up for a few seconds before going back to their original colors. You have to memorize the path across. (And if you've got the memory of a goldfish, you'll just have to follow the group.)

2 LONG JUMP

You can easily jump over a tile. Don't hesitate to join the other beans already on the way to victory by diving toward them. But when you get close to the other side, don't take too many risks (unless you're far behind).

3 ALWAYS FORWARD

You get to the finish line by never going back. Also, if you're on a tile that's lit up, the next safe one will either be on your left, your right, or in front of you. If you've spotted unstable tiles, it's easier to guess your next move. There are always two paths to get across at the start, but they merge before the finish line.

4 WATCH CLOSELY

Pay close attention when you are on the right track. You will see the fake tiles shake a little from time to time. This can help you figure out which way to go. So, if a tile on your left is shaking and the one in front of you is too, you know you can go to the one on your right. Keep those eyes peeled!

5 HOLD ON

You'll often find yourself on the same tile as many other beans. Hold on to them so you don't get pushed onto a fake tile. Even better, you can push an opponent to the edge of the tile you're on to test an adjacent tile without taking the risk yourself. Sure, it's mean . . . but it works.

6 FINAL SPRINT

You may have noticed that the course is made up of ten rows of ten tiles. When you get close to the end, remember that the way to the other side always has two tiles in a row straight toward the finish line. So, if you're on the second to last row, you can just go straight ahead before you jump to reach the finish line.

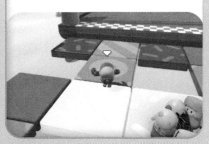

7 ALTERNATE VERSIONS

Occasionally, there are thicc bonkuses in this course. They move slowly, but they do make things harder—especially if they're between you and the finish line!

THE WHIRLYGIG

This round is perfect for training yourself to jump and dive in certain conditions. Here's what you need to remember.

1 FUN BEAMS

Travel in the same direction as the beam is rotating. You only have to jump to get over them, but if there are other beans around you, you can easily get thrown off balance. By moving with the beam rotation instead of against it, you can get propelled forward if you get hit.

2 PREPARE TO DIVE

When you reach the top of the yellow conveyor belt, jump and then dive to stay on the course. You can also grab the wall or jump on the small yellow barrier then jump forward to keep going. Just avoid jumping near another player or grabbing a wall if there's already player there. In some versions, a big yeetus appears above the conveyor belt, making the jump and dive a bit trickier.

3 FIRST SPIN

For the first set of spinning blades, wait for one of the blades to be on the left before moving forward. And watch out for the step. It's not high, but it can be hard to see. If you're not going absolutely straight ahead, you could trip and get knocked over by a blade. If you're lucky, the blade can lift you over the barrier, but don't count on it.

4 MORE PROPELLERS

These are easy. Go between two of them and watch out for that step. Sometimes there will be rotating hammers on the ground right after the blades, but there's enough space between the hammers for you to pass safely. There's also a chance that there will be thicc bonkuses instead of hammers.

5 DON'T RUN

Be careful here. Slow down a bit to get past the large spinning blades. Slowing down also allows you to stay in control and not fall down right after. This way, worst case, you'll stumble a bit and be able to keep going.

6 THE CONVEYOR BELT

You've got three options here. The first is to go straight to another conveyor belt that takes you under a set of fast-spinning blades. To have a chance of getting through, you have to dive at the right moment. But the speed of the blades makes this quite risky. You can try it if you are in the lead, but if it doesn't work, don't keep at it. Try going another way.

7 | OTHER WAYS

Whether you choose to go right or left, you have to go through a series of circular platforms and jump over a rotating beam. All you need to do to get to the platforms is jump. Avoid diving unless the rotating beam is about to hit you. You can move your camera overhead to get a better sense of distances here.

8 | FINAL DIVE

Plan your moves on the last platform so you put yourself to the left or the right of the blade. You can stay on the platform while you figure out your moves, but be sure to jump when the beam comes around. When you're ready, a jump followed by a dive will take you to the finish line.

9 | ALTERNATE VERSIONS

The circular platforms with the rotating beams right before the finish line are sometimes replaced by spinning plates. Fortunately, when that happens, the rotating beams are gone. Be extra careful when you jump!

BiG FANS

In this round, you have to jump on circular platforms shaped like fans. To reach the finish line, you'll have to be a professional jumper and diver.

1 TRAINING

You'll need to watch closely and use your skills in the first two parts of this course. You must jump and dive to get from one fan to the next. Be sure not to jump to the blade of a fan that's moving away from you, as you're likely to fall.

2 THE CROWD

As always, avoid crowds as much as you can. Other beans might push you off the platforms or prevent you from jumping properly. This is especially important in the second part of the race, where some fans have narrower blades than others.

3 NO LIMBO

In the last part of the course, the fans have a rotating beam that could knock you off at any point. While it rotates quite slowly, the beam itself is wide. One misstep and you'll end up getting unceremoniously tossed off.

FRUIT CHUTE

What happens when a bunch of beans try to go the wrong way on a conveyor belt? Bad things, especially when they have to dodge giant fruit! But it won't come to that if you follow these tips.

1 FIRST JUMP

When you jump to reach the conveyor belt, don't forget to dive so you avoid landing too close to the edge. This doesn't always work, so keep trying if you fail. The first pieces of fruit will start coming at you very quickly. With a little luck, you can leap over an orange and take the lead.

2 AVOID THE MIDDLE

Going up the middle of the conveyor belt is a bad idea. The fruit is shot from both sides, and it all tends to make its way to the middle of the belt. Then there are rolling logs that come down the belt, and smaller fruits (plums and strawberries) are often shot down the middle. If you want to improve your odds of finishing the course, go as far as you can to the right or left.

3 PROTECTION

On the sides of the conveyor belt, there are pink bumpers that can protect you. If a piece of fruit lands on one, it will often go over your head. You can situate your back to the bumpers if a piece of fruit is heading at you. This can help prevent you from getting pushed back too far.

4 THE FINISH

Like earlier in the course, don't go down the middle. A rolling log could knock you off your feet, and you don't want to end up back at the beginning. Stay on your toes until you get to the blue section.

5 ALTERNATE VERSIONS

The cannons sometimes shoot only one type of fruit (like watermelons or bananas), which can make getting up that conveyor belt even harder. And sometimes, right at the start of the conveyor belt, there are two big yeetuses. You might be tempted to use them to get up the conveyor belt faster than other players, but it's a risky move!

WALL GUYS

This is the perfect round for beans that love to climb. You have to go over three walls by climbing on blocks. As you might imagine, the blocks are a bit too small to accommodate everyone. This is a round where you've got to look out for yourself!

1 AGILE BEANS

The keys to success in this round are jumping, diving, and grabbing the edges of blocks and walls. Depending on the distance between you and the wall or block, you will have to jump, then dive and grab the ledge. Whenever you jump, be sure you're facing the wall or block head-on. And keep pressing the grab button until you've managed to climb onto the wall or block.

2 AVOID THE CROWDS

Most of the players will take the most obvious way over the wall, and the crowds will make jumping harder. You'll fall often when you try to grab and hang on to a block. You can also fall when you miss a jump due to another player pushing you. And if a player dives into you, they can knock you off a block or a wall you're holding on to before you even manage to climb it. If there are too many players in one place, it's best to go somewhere else.

3 MOVING THE BLOCKS

You can move blocks by grabbing them, as long as there aren't too many players on them. If that's the case, you'll need some other beans to help you. If one route up the wall is too crowded with other players, use your time to move other blocks around and make another path over the wall. You can also move blocks around to slow down other players.

4 IT'S IN GEAR!

In this course, you'll see some yellow gears to the side of the walls. After a little while, they start to turn, causing the walls to lower very slowly. Remember this. It will make getting over the last wall a lot easier.

5 SUCH GREAT HEIGHTS

There are different-sized blocks in this course. To reach the last wall, you don't have to climb the tallest one. You can jump, then dive and grab to pull yourself up onto the smaller ones.

6 USE OTHERS

Once you're over a wall, you can often jump on the tallest blocks without having to make your way up using smaller ones. If you're on a block that's a good height but that's a little too far away to reach the next wall, you can just wait for other players to push the block you're on. Work smarter, not harder!

KNIGHT FEVER

Bean life ain't easy. In this round you'll have to avoid swinging axes, spike logs, and thicc bonkuses that can slow you down or toss you off the course. Get ready to rumble!

1 CURVED PLATFORMS

The two places where you're most likely to fall in this course are the curved platforms. You'll encounter the first one at the start of the race, but the second is most likely to trip you up. Watch out for the holes in the platform—you can easily fall through. Try to keep your balance.

2 AXES

Don't worry! These axes won't chop you in half. They will, however, knock you right off the course. They're pretty thin so it can be hard to tell how far you are from the blade. Use your camera to shift your perspective and see if you can make it past.

3 LOGS

To make it over the spike logs, try moving your camera so it's above your bean. That way, you can get some perspective on the distance between you and the pink spikes. It's okay to take your time weaving safely between the spikes. Avoid the logs where there are lots of other players. It's common to fall when another bean pushes you toward a spike. The crowd, as usual, is your worst enemy.

4 SLIP AND SLIDE

Just after the spike logs, there's a big slime-covered hill that will make you go really fast. To reduce the likelihood of getting hit by the axes, try to aim between two axes. And do your best to slow down at the end so you don't fall on your way to the thicc bonkuses.

5 THICC BONKUSES

These huge, long rollers are covered in spikes. To get past them, you've got to travel along the sides of the course. You can try to go through the middle, but you'll probably get hit and wind up pushed into a hole. Be careful not to knock into other players when you're on the platform sides. That curved platform makes it easy to fall. And remember, you can always dive to avoid getting dragged off by the thicc bonkuses.

6 THE DRAWBRIDGES

This last part of the course isn't too hard. Just aim for the drawbridge that's at its steepest and you'll get there when it's lowered. In some versions, the drawbridges don't completely lower and there are axes either before or in the middle of the bridges.

7 ALTERNATE VERSIONS

In other versions, the spike logs are replaced by seesaws. Swinging axes in the middle of these platforms make players go to one side and that makes the seesaw tilt precariously.

TUNDRA RUN

Snowballs, icy platforms, blizzard fans, and flippers—this is a tricky round! It's time to put on your mittens and focus.

1 THE CORNERS

As you can imagine, it's going to get crowded when you go around those first two corners. Snowball cannons fire at regular intervals: one ball on the left, one ball on the right. Jump over the small obstacles to avoid weaving and keep traveling in a straight line. This is the best way to get to the next part in the course quickly. And be careful, the snowballs keep getting bigger as they roll.

2 FISTICUFFS

You can go straight when you're on icy platforms, but you'll have to dodge the punching gloves! If you get hit, best-case scenario, they'll knock you down—worst-case scenario, they'll throw you off the course.

3 ANOTHER WAY

You can avoid the icy surface by dropping to the right or left of the course. You'll be falling from high up, so be sure to dive before you land to avoid losing too much time. There are two punching gloves on the sides down here, but you should have enough space to go safely between them.

4 IT'S WINDY!

If you've managed to keep your footing on the icy paths and the punching gloves didn't knock you out, you can take advantage of the blizzard fans to get propelled forward onto the red platforms. But be careful, those platforms are actually punching gloves, and they can send you flying!

5 ICY PATHS

Instead of passing the punching gloves to reach the next part of the course, you can use the icy paths off to the sides. Be careful to avoid the bumpers. If you're near other players, you can mess with them by grabbing them to slow them down or make them change direction.

6 HEADWINDS

Before you can cross the finish line, you have to squeeze between the green flippers and avoid the powerful gusts from the blizzard fans on the sides of the course. The safest way to get through this section is to stand with your back to the icy wall and walk in a straight line to get safely behind the fans. Be careful, if you step on a flipper, it will throw you backward.

7 JUMPING BEAN

To reach the finish line, you have to go over two green flippers that will propel you forward. Try to not use the flippers in the middle or you might fall into the void. You're better off using the ones on either side. Watch out: when a player uses the flipper, it can take a second before it's ready to launch a bean again. With practice, you can bounce off both in a single jump and cross the finish line.

FREEZY PEAK

This round will blow you away! You'll have to cross the finish line using the blizzard fans to reach new heights. Watch out for the final climb—it'll make you a dizzy bean!

1 START DIFFERENT

This round is not the same for every bean at the start. You might find yourself facing red platforms (watch out: those are punching gloves!) or green flippers. The main difference is that if you start with punching gloves, you won't have to dodge snowballs fired by cannons.

2 HARD KNOCKS

In the first part of the course, you want to stay in the middle as much as you can. Watch out for the two punching gloves that might slow you down and for the blizzard fan that's right after the flippers. You might get blown back on the flippers then launched even farther back.

3 CONVEYOR BELT

The cannons in front of the conveyor belt shoot snowballs left and right. Try to go around them. And no matter what, don't jump or dive. One misstep and you could find yourself back where you started.

4 DON'T FALL

When you get to the first blizzard fan that blows you up to the next level, be careful not to fall back on the flippers. They'll throw you backward and you'll waste more time.

5 BEANS IN THE WILD

Jump over to the gust of wind and hold your bean right over the first blizzard fan before moving toward the next. You have to allow your bean to get high enough to reach the rest of the course. Watch out: If you come into contact with another bean, you might get thrown off balance with disastrous consequences. Occasionally, you'll find snowballs way up here, but they don't usually get in the way.

6 IT'S STEEP!

Once you've made it up the stairs, you have to get past the punching gloves that'll push you onto the flippers. If you're unlucky, those flippers will shoot you right off the course. If you're lucky, they'll just push you into one of the big snowballs rolling down on the left, and you'll get knocked out. It's best to stay in the middle and jump then dive over the flippers. If this is too hard, weave between the flippers and the snowballs, moving past the punching gloves when they're already extended.

7 CONVEYOR BELTS

Once you've gotten past the punching gloves, jump on the first conveyor belt and make your way up to the last blizzard fan. Since it can be a bit disorienting, use your camera to figure out the way to the finish line so you don't end up falling back when you dive.

SLIME CLIMB

Beware, little bean, this round will test your patience. The course has ten sections, and each one will challenge your control and your nerve. And all the while, the slime keeps getting deeper!

1 YELLOW BUMPER

At the start, try to jump on the yellow bumper under the green and yellow moving blocks. Watch out: the moving blocks can push you right back off. But don't be stubborn. If your first attempt doesn't work, follow the ramp instead. The slime level rises faster than you'd think.

2 BOMBS AWAY!

There are no obstacles on this ramp itself, but you've got to dodge giant balls or logs as wide as the entire ramp, depending on what the cannon is shooting. Getting hit can have fatal consequences. If you're facing the logs head-on, jump at just the right moment and go to the right to take the shortcut to the fourth ramp. If the cannon is shooting at you, try to position yourself to the left to continue up the ramp without getting hit. (But keep an eye out for other beans!)

3 THE MOVING BLOCKS

These two moving blocks take the entire width of the ramp. They don't move in sync, so try to jump when you see the second block retracting. By the time you get past the first block, the second one will have cleared the path. Travel along the edge of the ramp to avoid getting hit by the moving block. If it looks like the first block is going to get you, jump and aim your camera at the second platform before diving down to land on it. But be careful—this is a difficult move to master.

4 THE CONVEYOR BELT

This ramp is a conveyor belt that will try to drag you to the ramp below. To avoid this, move to the right of the ramp, toward the yellow beams. Be sure to jump out of the way when the donut bumpers are about to get you. As long as you take your time on this part of the course, you should reach the next part with no problem.

5 THE BEAM BRIDGE

Make your way along the beam less traveled to avoid getting pushed around by your rivals. Avoid jumping to reach the first beam, and stay balanced in the center. Then jump to the second beam. Aim for the middle of the ramp as you make your way across the next beam. Sometimes, mischievous players hang out on the second beam to knock off other players. You can jump and dive to avoid these mean beans. If you try to beat them at their own game by pushing them aside, you might end up falling.

6 UNDER THE HAMMER

This ramp is covered in slime. Not only does it slow you down but it gets slippery if you jump. Your best bet is to make your way up the ramp by walking diagonally to the right. Go between the rotating hammers so they don't hit you. After you make your way across the beams, you can jump up to the next ramp (as pictured) to save some time. If you're feeling gutsy, you can also try hopping on a hammer for a shortcut. (See tip 11.)

7 THE MOVING BLOCKS ARE BACK!

This time, there are four moving blocks. But you don't need to jump over them. You should still travel along the right side of the ramp to avoid getting knocked down. And if you're uneasy, take your time. You can position your camera off to the side to better gauge the distance between you and the blocks.

8 BUMPERS + SLIME = DANGER

News flash: the slime is slippery. Go up the ramp diagonally from left to right to avoid issues. Be sure to slow down when you need to dodge a donut bumper. If you don't, it could spell disaster. Play around with your camera to get a better sense of your position relative to the bumpers.

9 THE FINISH LINE!

You'll still be in the slime in the last part of this course, and you'll have to dodge three pendulums. Sometimes there are big yeetuses instead of pendulums, and sometimes there's a thicc bonkus. As before, camera control is key—use it to gauge your distance from these obstacles so they don't whack you. The finish line is just ahead!

10 FOR THE TRUE VILLAINS

If you're ahead of the pack, you can wait for other players and try to grab them while they're still in the slime. Then you can push them back to make them slip backward or—even better—get knocked on the head. It may be cruel, but it means you've got fewer beans to compete with on the next level! And admit it. . . . It's fun.

11 SHORTCUTS

If you're feeling gutsy, you can try taking a few shortcuts. For example, you can jump just after the beam bridge to reach the ramp with the hammers, then jump on the first hammer all the way to the right. This will help you avoid the ramp with the three moving blocks. The move takes a lot of practice, but it can be quite effective.

SKI FALL

To qualify, you have to collect fifteen points as fast as you can by passing through holes in the spinning wheels and the bullseye at the end. The icy, sloping course makes this the fastest round in *Fall Guys*.

1 THE LORD OF THE RINGS

Depending on the position of the rings in each wheel, you'll have to choose between jumping, diving, or both. When the hole you want to jump through is near the bottom of the wheel, be sure to dive and not jump. If you jump, you could bump your head on the wheel and fall into the void. The bronze rings are worth one point, the silver are worth two points, and the gold are worth five points.

2 WINNER BEAN

It's possible to make it into the gold ring at the end! If you can, head for the springboard. It'll help you gain enough momentum to get through the gold ring. With practice, you'll be able to get more than ten points in a single trip!

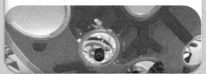

3 FAST & FURIOUS

The icy, sloped course makes beans travel at the speed of light! Good aim is key. More daring beans can travel along the sides to go straight for the final ring, and you've only got to do that three times to qualify!

4 SPRINGBOARDS

To make sure you get through the gold ring at the end of the course, use one of the three springboards. Don't forget to dive if you need to adjust your trajectory. The blizzard fans can affect your jump.

5 TOSSED BEAN

Watch out when you're on your way to the last ring. There are flippers on the course that can throw you off. Getting thrown off the course doesn't eliminate you, but it brings you back to the beginning of the course, prevents you from getting points from that last wheel, and slows you down.

6 THE END

At the end of the course, you have to jump into the void. But that's okay. You respawn at the start of the course until you've hit fifteen points or the number of qualified beans reaches it first. Try to jump through the center of the bullseye to get five points. If you land on the pink arrows, there's a small chance you'll bounce off them and into the gold ring!

7 GET IT RIGHT

The first wheel only has one gold ring, and you can't get to it when you're initially traveling downhill. However, there's a flipper on the course just after the wheel that you can use to propel yourself backward and into the hole. It's a long shot, but it's possible!

JUMP CLUB

This round is all on one single platform hovering above a pool of slime. You have to jump over a beam that keeps spinning faster, all while avoiding a second larger beam. If you don't time it just right, you're toast.

1 YOUR CAMERA

In this round, your camera is your best friend. You want to keep it moving so you can see where the lower beam is. The larger rotating beam above tends to conceal the lower one, preventing you from planning your jumps.

2 PICK A SPOT

Like other rounds, it's best to pick a spot with few players. That way, you're less likely to get caught or to fall when landing a jump. Players will also try to prevent you from jumping over the beam, which can knock you down and eliminate you. What's worse, there are cannons shooting fruit in some versions, making it even more crowded and dangerous.

3 AVOID DIVING

When the two rotating beams are aligned, you can't jump. You'd be pushed back by the top beam, then thrown off the platform by the bottom. When this happens, don't try to dive. Just walk ahead of the beams in the direction they're spinning until they separate enough for you to jump.

BLOCK PARTY

In this round, you're on a platform with a bunch of blocks moving across it, and you need to avoid getting chucked into the slime. Losing is bad—but the smell is worse.

1 CAN'T STOP, WON'T STOP

The key to this round is to keep moving. This is especially important when long blocks force you to travel all the way from one side of the platform to the other to avoid getting pushed off.

2 THE WOODEN BEAMS

Halfway through the round, a series of blocks connected by a wooden beam will hurdle toward you. Hop over the beam or you'll get swept away! Avoid jumping near others— you might fall and get hit by the next block. This part of the round is nearly over when the blocks take up almost the entire platform, forcing everyone to jump through a small gap.

3 BLOCK WALL

The last part of the round will make all the players crowd together and navigate obstacles in close quarters. Try to stay away from the back of the platform. That way, you'll have time to get back up if you fall. In some versions, you have to weave around walls or jump over more wooden beams.

ROLL OUT

This round will test your balance. You have to stay on top of the five rotating rings that move in different directions. Each ring has bumpers, holes, and walls that force you to switch between them.

1 IN BETWEEN

One of the safest strategies is to start on the blue ring—it rotates the slowest. To keep your balance, you should go from the blue to the purple, then from the purple back to the blue.

2 PERSPECTIVE

Like in other rounds, you can use your camera to get some perspective. You can look at what's going on around you and make sure you're not about to drop into the slime below. But beware, it's pretty easy to lose your sense of direction and confuse which way the roller is turning.

3 PUSH OTHERS

Once you have a bit more experience, it can be tempting to grab another bean when they're near a gap in the roller and to try to push them in. This can be risky, because the other bean might try to return the favor. If you're playing as a team, choose an isolated opponent and go after them together in order to have a better chance of heaving them off.

4 ALTERNATE VERSIONS

Sometimes the rings on the end disappear, making things much more crowded. And that can quickly lead to a cascade of beans. Other times, you have to deal with fruit cannons shooting strawberries and plums your way.

PERFECT MATCH

ROUND TYPE
LOGIC

How sharp is your memory? As sharp as a teddy bear, you say? Well that's too bad, because in this round you have just a few seconds to remember the position of the fruit icons on the tiles underfoot. You then have to run to the tiles that match the fruit on the big screen. It may be straightforward, but it isn't easy.

1 IN BETWEEN

At the beginning, you only have to memorize two fruit icons. This is simple enough that you can simultaneously get rid of an opponent who is close to the edge. If you're playing as a team, you can gang up on an unsuspecting neighbor. Having two of you grab an opponent means a better chance of sending them off to a slimy fate.

2 PERSPECTIVE

Use your camera to get a good view of all the tiles. Try to memorize an entire row or a set of four adjacent tiles. This will make the rest of this round easier. If you can't remember where you should go, follow the other beans to the most crowded tile.

3 PUSH OTHERS

If you're on a tile with a herd of opponents and they try to push you off, grab them and hang on for dear life. But watch out—accidents happen and they happen fast!

4 FAKE OUT

This tactic is risky, and it's best to reserve it for the third round. If you notice a lot of players following you to the right tiles, you can go to a wrong one, then dive off it to the right one at the last second. The beans that followed you could fall for your trap and into the slime.

5 ALTERNATE VERSIONS

Many players found this round too easy, so the game developers added a rotating beam. It moves slowly, but it makes things a bit more confusing. You have to memorize the tile icons while also jumping regularly to keep your footing.

HOOPSIE LEGENDS

ROUND TYPE
HUNT

This is a perfect round for agile beans. You'll need good jumping, diving, and observation skills to qualify. And, as with most other events, you've got to keep your cool.

1 THE RINGS

In this round, rings appear very regularly all over the place, and you'll need to pass through them in order to score points. When you start, use your camera to figure out which ones are closest to you. White rings are worth one point, and gold rings are worth five points (but they're usually harder to reach). You have to get six points to qualify.

2 GLOBAL STRATEGY

The best way to have a good overview of the arena is to go near the continually rising drawbridges. To get there, move one of the many boxes that are scattered around. You'll then be high enough to jump and dive your way through the rings.

3 Gold Rings

As a general rule, don't waste time trying to jump through the gold rings at the edges of the arena (aside from the gold rings near or in the middle of the drawbridges). You often have to use a crate to reach them, and there will be lots of players gathering around them to try their luck. You'll spend more time on them than you'd expect.

4 The Accessible Rings

On the edges of the arena, you'll see white rings appear regularly near the platforms. You can get through them with a simple jump. Keep an eye out for them, and move quickly when they show up. If you're close by when they appear, these rings are pretty easy to collect.

5 Alternate Versions

In some versions, there are no drawbridges, which means you haveto use blocks to get up high.

And sometimes there are swinging axes near the drawbridges and around the platforms at the edges.

TAIL TAG

Noobs will likely find this round frustrating. But with these tips and a little bit of practice, you'll be a pro in no time.

1 STARTING WITHOUT A TAIL

If you start the game without a tail, you're a hunter. Take a good look around to spot the players with tails. Try to find ways to cut them off instead of running after them. If you notice a player with a tail doing risky jumps, stalk them for a few seconds and keep an eye out for any misstep.

2 STARTING WITH A TAIL

If you start with a tail, go to the platforms in the center leading to the rotating hammer. As soon as a player without a tail approaches, jump to another platform. If you don't feel confident doing this, you can jump and dive to be sure you make it.

3 MOVE THE CAMERA

One of the keys to success is constantly moving your camera to track what's happening around you. Whether you are hunting or being hunted, this gives you the perspective to know whether you need to attack or run.

4 JUMP, DIVE, GRAB

Jumping, diving, and then grabbing a bean with a tail is a good strategy, so long as you have good aim. But if you don't manage to grab them, you'll lose time getting up. Use this tactic as a last resort if you don't have a tail, there's a player with one in range, and the round is about to end.

5 THE CENTRAL HAMMER

Some players with a tail will take cover underneath the rotating hammer. To get to the center, you have to dive at just the right time. It's not a perfect hiding place, but if players without tails come after you, you can always jump into the hammer's path and get it to launch you beyond the reach of your pursuers.

6 THE END IN SIGHT

When there are ten seconds left in the round, if you've got a tail, you should use your camera, find the place where there are the fewest players, and make a break for it. Go to the outer edges of the arena if it's less crowded, but just get as far from players without tails as you can.

7 SNATCH

If there are about twenty seconds left and you still don't have a tail, use your camera to find a bean with a target then go cut them off. Look out for beans jumping from platform to platform. They make excellent candidates for tail theft. When you get a tail, you can jump and dive so they don't steal it right back.

8 HAMMERED

If you have a tail with only a few seconds left on the clock and you're close to other players without a tail, you can try getting hit by a rotating hammer. Some will throw you so high that nobody will be able to reach you. Best of all, when you get hit (or knock into it when jumping and then fall), you get half a second when no one can steal your tail. That moment can mean the difference between a furry qualification or shuffling home, tailless.

ROCK 'N' ROLL

Pushing a big ball together toward a goal might sound simple, but it's anything but. You've also got to prevent others from getting there first, which means this round gets messy pretty quickly.

1 PUSH TOGETHER

During the first part of the round, you have to push the ball along a corridor full of obstacles meant to block you and slow you down. Your team has to work together to move the ball quickly around the obstacles and up the slope leading to the goal.

2 THE SCOUT

When you're halfway down the corridor, a player should go forward to the final slope to keep an eye on how the other teams are doing. That player can also start trying to hinder another team by getting in front of their balls.

3 THE LAST OBSTACLE

On the slope toward the goal, there can be rotating hammers, bumpers, or pendulums. These can be quite tricky. But no matter the version, you'll need a group of players to make sure your ball gets in the goal. More often than not, that means playing rough.

EGG SCRAMBLE

ROUND TYPE
TEAM

The egg hunt is on! Each team has to put as many eggs as possible in their nest before time runs out. But there aren't enough eggs to go around!

1 THE BEGINNING

At first, it's a free-for-all. When you go to grab the eggs, rather than bringing the eggs back to your nest, throw them behind you, between the curved wall and the nest. That way your teammates can collect the eggs and bring them to the nest, where they'll have the wall protecting them.

2 THROW THE EGGS

Whenever you've got an egg, jump and dive in the direction of your nest, dropping the egg to throw it. This method can work extremely well if your teammates are there to catch them.

3 GOLDEN EGGS

The golden eggs can tip the scales in your favor. These beauties are worth five points and are coveted by all beans. But you can't rely on them alone. While they're important, that also means if you lose one, you're down five points. Make sure your nest is full of all kinds of eggs, not just the shiny ones. In some versions of this round, however, all the eggs are golden eggs. This shouldn't change your strategy, but it will certainly change your scores!

4 DEFEND YOUR NEST

When your team gets over ten points, you should focus on defending your nest and making sure beans from opposing teams don't come help themselves to your hard-earned eggs. The best strategy is to stay in the nest. If you have a golden egg, keep hold of it. As soon as an opponent enters the nest, grab them to slow them down. If they try to steal an egg, make them drop it.

5 SPOT THE WEAK TEAM

If you notice a team having a hard time, try to prevent them from bringing eggs to their nest, or go help yourself to their eggs. To win this round, the most important thing is simply to not be the team with the fewest eggs.

FALL BALL

L ots of beans like to play soccer, so a round was created just for them! Only there are a couple of problems: there are two balls and they're three times as tall as the beans! Here are some tips that'll make this round easier.

1 BALL TYPES

In most versions, the beans are playing with soccer balls. But sometimes a rugby ball appears instead. As you might imagine, it doesn't bounce as predictably. Other times it's a golden egg that appears instead of a ball, and scoring a goal with that gets you five points!

2 OBSTACLES

The arena might contain a number of obstacles that will impact the way that you play. There are sometimes pendulums in front of the goals that will get in the way. Rotating hammers can help you either defend your goal or score a goal depending on how you use them. Occasionally there's also a spinning plate in the middle of the arena that you can use to pick up speed— either for yourself or for a ball.

3 DEFENSE

No matter how many beans are on a team, you need at least one bean playing defense. If you're playing defense, try to get a sense of the distance between yourself, the balls, and the players of the opposing team.

This way you can, for example, avoid getting too close and having the ball go over your head. As soon as your team has scored one or two more goals than the other team, focus on defense until the end of the game.

4 SHIRT PULLING

Pulling an opponent's shirt is a valid play here. When you see a bean from another team approaching the ball, you can slow them down by grabbing them. Sometimes it's more helpful to slow down attackers than to rush for the ball.

TEAM TAIL TAG

This round usually comes up when there are enough beans for four teams. The team that finishes with the fewest tails is eliminated!

1 STAY HIGH

One of the best strategies is to keep to the higher platforms. You can avoid the rotating hammers and yeetuses there by jumping and diving. By staying up high, you'll have a better vantage point, and, if you have a tail, you'll be able to escape other beans more easily. If you're after a tail, staying up high means you'll be waiting in the spots that players with tails are trying to reach!

2 THE COUNTER

Keep an eye on how many tails your team has. If you see your team is in the lead and you don't have a tail yet, you can focus on slowing down players of opposing teams by grabbing them. And if you have a hard time staying away from beans on the other teams in general, you can support your team by focusing on slowing down your opponents.

3 FAST ESCAPE

If you have a bunch of beans chasing you, you can head for the conveyor belt. If you drop onto it properly, it will help you move away quickly and climb up to safety. You can also try to hide among players from opposing teams that have tails, since they are as likely as you are to have their tails stolen.

4 HIDING OUT

You'll notice that beans with a tail often end up near the rotating hammers. If you have a tail and can shelter behind the hammer's range, players who try to attack you are likely to get hit, launching them far, far away. If they do manage to make it through, you often have time to escape. Remember, you can use hammers to get thrown far away too.

JINXED

Two teams, each with a jinxed bean . . . To win this round, you have to jinx the most beans on the opposing team before time runs out. Get ready for chaos!

1 WHEN YOU'RE JINXED

Whenever you get jinxed, try to cut off beans on the opposing team as often as you can. All you have to do is catch an opponent to jinx them. (A jinxed bean looks like they're surrounded by a pink cloud.) Don't forget to use your camera to quickly spot your next target.

2 WHEN YOU'RE NOT JINXED

If you're not jinxed at the start of the game, keep your eye on the jinxed bean on the opposing team so you can avoid them. You can help your team by grabbing opponents who aren't jinxed to help one of the jinxed members of your team to jinx them. Do your best to not trip in this round.

3 THE SPINNING PLATES

The spinning plates can help yougain speed and outrun your opponents. Try to go there at the start of the round if there aren't any jinxed players from the other team.

And be sure to adjust your camera so you can keep an eye out for jinxed beans who might be out to get you.

4 AVOID THE TRENCHES

In the center, there is a trench with pendulums swinging over it regularly. This is the danger zone.

The pendulums can make things confusing, and it's easy for your enemies to corner you.

HOARDERS

With seven balls and three teams, there's bound to be a fight! Like all team rounds, one group is going to be left out. Here's what you need to make sure it's not you.

1 MANDATORY DEFENSE

Once your team has brought three balls back to your area (preferably near the walls), it's time for defense. Find somewhere elevated in your area and stay ready to headbutt the ball if an enemy bean tries to steal it. Pay attention and react as soon as you see more than one bean from another team starting to push one of your balls.

2 OBSTACLES

In some versions, there might be rotating hammers or donut bumpers. These can help you in both defense and offense. Remember, it's important to maintain your defense once your team has collected several balls.

3 HELP YOUR OPPONENT

When two teams are tied, the game adds overtime seconds—and sometimes those seconds can change the outcome of a game. So if there's a battle between two teams behind you, you can push balls over to one of the opposing teams in order to end the game while you're ahead.

EGG SIEGE

This round looks a lot like Egg Scramble, except the nests are harder to reach. Here's how you protect your coop!

1 DIVE AND RELEASE

The beans that go grab the eggs from the center have to quickly dive and then release their eggs to throw them toward their waiting teammates. This strategy is even more important in this round since the nests are farther away. If you are close to the center, you should grab and throw the eggs. If you are farther out, you should collect the thrown eggs and bring them to the nest.

2 DEFEND

There should always be one or two beans on your team to protect your nest and preventing opponents from stealing your eggs. Even if your nest is empty, you should stay there to slow down your rivals.

3 ATTACK

Like in other rounds, keep an eye on the opposing teams' scores. You'll want to go steal eggs from the team with the lowest score. What's important is qualifying, not having the most eggs. You can jump and dive to eject an egg from a hostile nest, or you can carry it away by hand.

Hoopsie Daisy

ROUND TYPE
TEAM

I n this round, your team has to jump through as many rings as possible. Like most team events, only two teams will qualify. It's time to be nimble and quick.

1 HOLD YOUR GROUND

Use your camera to keep an eye out for the rings, as well as beans from other teams. You can use it to gauge the distance between you, your target ring, and your opponents. There's no point running to a ring that's far away. The rings appear regularly, so it's smarter to pick a small area in which to score points instead of running around without contributing to your team's score.

2 GOLD PLATED

There are occasionally gold rings that show up. You should know by now what that means: a great opportunity to get five points. But don't waste too much time chasing gold rings. Steadily collecting points is what's important.

3 RAMPS

Position yourself near the ramps (at the edges or in in the middle). Many rings tend to appear up high, including those coveted gold ones. But you'll often be fighting with other beans to get to them. Don't hesitate to grab your opponents before they start jumping toward a ring. Doing this means you might make them miss, and you're more likely to grab the prize.

SNOWY SCRAP

Some players dread team rounds, because there's a chance you'll end up with incompetent beanmates. Here's what you need to know to quickly find your role in a team—but no matter what, don't give up, and change roles if you need to.

1 LET IT ROLL

To win, you need to roll your snowball over one hundred hexagons of snow. The snowball keeps getting bigger . . . and harder to push. You've got to roll up your sleeves and work as a team to qualify.

2 CAMERA

Keep moving your camera to find the places with the most snow. After a snowball rolls over the snow, it will take a few seconds for the snow to appear again. Moving your camera around also lets you locate the other teams.

3 PUNCHING GLOVES

Pushing your snowball over to the punching gloves is a good idea. When the glove punches the snowball, it'll propel it toward the center of the arena, allowing the ball to roll quickly over a lot of snow.

4 IT'S HEAVY!

By the time your team reaches 75 percent, the ball will be much bigger and harder to move. Your whole team has to work together at this point if you want to win, so there's no longer time to go bugging the other teams.

5 BLOCK OTHERS

Just like in Rock 'n' Roll, one or two players from your team should try to slow down another team. To do this, get on the other side of their snowball and try to direct it to places without snow.

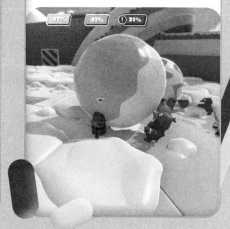

6 WHEN BEANS ATTACK

If you see a player from another team on the way to block your team's snowball, go grab them to slow them down. If you do it right, they could quickly get bored and return to their team or move on to another team's snowball.

PEGWIN PURSUIT

In this round, teams have to hold pegwins for as long as possible ... but there are just two pegwins for three teams! You can do anything to win (but only to other beans)!

1 CAMERA

It's important to have a good view of the arena in this round. Use your camera to make sure you always have one of the two pegwins in your sights. When a pegwin is nearby, place the camera just above your head so you can follow it more easily.

2 LET GO

If one of your opponents is holding a pegwin, grab them to make them drop it. Then one of your teammates can snatch it up. You can also grab an opponent to prevent them from attacking someone on your team. Your score goes up one point for every second someone on your team is holding a pegwin.

3 BODYGUARD

In this round, there are two pegwins wandering about. If you get one of them, try to get as far away from the crowd as possible. If a teammate can go with you to watch your back, you'll be safer. They can prevent opponents from grabbing you while you rack up points.

ROLL OFF

This final round is a version of Roll Out. Even if you think you've mastered it, don't get too cocky. The rotating rings speed up, making it easy to lose your balance.

1 ON THE EDGE

In this round, you should move regularly from one ring to another so you don't fall off. The safest thing to do is to stay near the center, allowing you to easily move from one ring to the next.

2 AGAINST THE FLOW

At first, the rings spin slowly enough that you can stay on them as long as you move in the opposite direction. When there's a hole, you can jump and dive to get over. You only want to jump when there's a wall, though, otherwise you might fall off.

3 HOLD ON

You can get a little aggressive and grab another player to keep them from jumping for a bit. And when the rings speed up, you can easily take out an opponent with a grab.

4 DIVING OR JUMPING

When the rings spin faster, it's often better to dive instead of jumping from ring to ring. This will keep you closer to the ground. And move your camera so you stay near the top of the rings as much as possible. It's easy to get confused once things speed up!

FALL MOUNTAIN

A lot of players dread this final round. It's unforgiving. Remember these tips to help you become the king of the mountain.

1 AT THE START

You'll start on a platform that ends in a triangle. The best strategy is to jump straight ahead. If you're in the second row, you can go off the sides, but be sure you're perpendicular to the edge when you jump so you don't trip. When you're off the platform, come back to the center.

2 THE TURNSTILES

Head toward the turnstile on the right. Often, the first ball to fall hits this turnstile and spins it clockwise. If you're lucky, the turnstile will push you into the lead.

3 THE MIDDLE AISLE

Before picking which side of the course you want to climb, you should keep toward the center. Most of the balls bounce off the walls, but you should still pay attention and move out of the way if one comes at you. You won't get eliminated if a ball hits you, but it will certainly slow you down.

4 RIGHT OR LEFT?

Many players will head to the right of the course, though both paths are valid. Always look up ahead to see where the balls will fall. Whatever happens, get as close to the wall as possible (on either side) before you climb the stairs to the crown.

5 | HAMMERS

The safest way to get past the row of rotating hammers and reach the steps is to go along the wall. That way, you just have to avoid one hammer. And don't forget to jump right after so you don't trip on the first step.

6 | THE FINAL CLIMB

When you climb to the crown, always go to the side where the rotating hammer can hit you in the back. Worst-case scenario, it'll push you forward and you can keep going up. Do this again with the one right before the crown so you don't get knocked back if you get hit.

7 | THE CROWN

Never jump toward the crown when it's climbing (unless it's at its lowest). You're likely to miss it. If there are other players beside you, wait half a second, grab one, and immediately release them so they miss their jump. And don't forget to use the button to grab the crown when you land on it!

HEX-A-GONE

This round is considered one of the most technically challenging in the game. The disappearing floor doesn't help. You'll need to pay attention, be patient, and use all your skills to make it through.

1 YOUR CAMERA

You have to position your camera so you can see what's going on beneath you. If you don't get the angle right, you could fall through a number of floors at the same time. This is the most crucial tip to remember—even more important than keeping an eye on your opponents.

2 THE START

This final round can vary in difficulty depending on the number of players. If there are more than ten (it does happen) let yourself drop down at the start and avoid diving at all costs. If there are only a handful of players (eight or fewer), it can help to jump to the empty floor hexagons on the top level.

3 DELAY JUMPING

When you jump or step on a hexagon, it sinks a bit before it disappears. You have just under a second before you have to move to another one, or else you'll fall through. When there are no other players around, jump from one hexagon to the next, paying close attention to the time. This is the key to all victories.

4 THE FALL

Sometimes you won't have a choice, and you'll be forced to dive after a jump in order to reach a series of hexagons. Still, avoid diving when you fall from one floor to another where possible. Diving wastes precious time and often takes out two or three tiles.

5 CUT THEM OFF

You'll often end up on a floor with other beans. You can cut them off while simultaneously walking on as many hexagons as you like. You want to force any opponent who's following you to change direction or fall. Then you can delay jumping and stay on the same floor as long as possible.

6 GRABBING

If another player is right in front of you, you can try to grab them and quickly release them. This can make them fall (especially if they were about to jump). But remember: you'll have to jump right after that, or there's a good chance that you'll take a plunge too.

7 WHEN TO DIVE

Jumping followed by diving allows you to jump over two slabs. Doing this allows you to reach faraway tiles. With practice, you'll be able to gauge the distances between tiles better.

8 AIM FOR A FLOOR

You can't stay on one floor indefinitely. And you have to quickly identify which direction you should go to land on the floor below you. The positioning of your camera can make a big difference here. It takes time to master this move, but with practice you'll get the hang of it.

9 DROPPING ALL THE WAY

You may have read that the ultimate trick is to drop to the lowest floor and step on as many hexagons as possible so the other players have nothing to land on. This isn't actually a good idea. You'll notice experienced players hang out on the upper levels as long as they can, meaning you'd run out of hexagons to jump on. That and a lot of random things need to align for this strategy to work, meaning it's not very effective.

ROYAL FUMBLE

ROUND TYPE
FINAL

This final round is just like Team Tail Tag except that there's only one tail and only one player can win. Here are some tips for navigating the arena, and you can return to Team Tail Tag for tips on getting the tail.

1 CLIMB UP HIGH

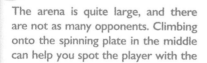

The arena is quite large, and there are not as many opponents. Climbing onto the spinning plate in the middle can help you spot the player with the tail. You want to try to cut them off, and climbing high allows you to see well enough to figure out a battle plan.

2 HUNTED OR HUNTER

As soon as you get the tail, all the other players are gunning for you. Use your camera to spot who's coming your way. Avoid the reverse conveyor belts, and use the ramps to reach the large spinning plate. That way, you'll be able to more easily outrun your pursuers, using the plate to gain momentum and jumping to a less populated part of the arena.

3 AVOID FALLING

This may sound obvious, but it bears repeating. If you have the tail, you have to go from the large spinning plate to the ramps, then use the small spinning plate to maintain distance between you and your pursuers. If you need to, you can go down into the arena and try to climb up another ramp farther away. Remember to always land on level ground so you don't trip and fall.

JUMP SHOWDOWN

Remember Jump Club? This round is similar, except for one big difference. The platform sections beneath players disappear until there are only two left. And just like with the other final rounds, there's only one winner!

1 A Fun Beam

The rotating beam you have to jump over crosses the entire platform this time, so you've got to plan two jumps. Of course, you want to avoid bumping your head on the big foam beam above that rotates at a different speed. With each new rotation, the lower beam spins faster and faster.

2 It's Shaking!

When a section of the platform starts to shake, you have a limited amount of time to move to another section before it disappears. Depending on where you are on this section, you have to quickly choose a direction, while simultaneously predicting when the rotating beams will get to you.

3 PLACE YOURSELF

As the round progresses, you can't move around as much. Sections of the platform disappear randomly until there are just two remaining. Until that happens, try to stay in the area with the most sections. You shouldn't ever be on a platform that is two sections apart from other remaining platforms—that leaves you unable to jump to safety if your section is about to disappear.

4 DIVE

There may come a time when you'll have to dive, like if you have to move to a part of the platform where there are more adjacent tiles or if you need to get away from other players, both of which can increase your chances of winning. When you need to dive or jump, do it in the same direction the beam is rotating to decrease your chances of getting swiped by it. Stand on the edge of the platform section, jump, and then dive when you're at your highest point.

5 EXPERIENCE

Be sure to use all the tips from Jump Club so you can win! Try to remember to grab opponents from time to time so they fall on the beams.

THIN ICE

When there's a bunch of beans on an iceberg, things get hot and the ice melts pretty quickly. As usual, only one bean can win. Use these tips to help keep your footing.

1 BREAK THE ICE

When you are on a hexagon of ice, it cracks. You can stay on it for about three seconds before it disappears. The arena has three layers of ice. Just like in Hex-A-Gone, you have to keep moving and learn to delay your jumps so you don't break the ice too quickly.

2 BEANS IN A HURRY

Take your time at the start of the game. Some beans will run around and crack as much ice as they can, but nothing is preventing you from staying in one part of the arena, delaying your jumps, and observing their behavior. This way you can spot the most dangerous or experienced players from the start.

3 THE BEAN TRAP

At the outset of the game, you can have fun melting the first two layers of ice and starting to work on the last in order to trap your opponents. If you use this strategy in a bunch of places, some clumsy beans could quickly find themselves trapped.

4 ON THE EDGES

Keep an eye on the other players. When you see a bean wandering around the edges of the iceberg, you can try to grab them and give them a good shove. An unprepared player could get eliminated quickly. Even if you can't push the player off, you can still distract them!

5 YOUR CAMERA

Are you sensing a pattern with this tip? The more the game progresses, the more important it is to keep track of the safer parts of the iceberg. Identify secure areas, delay your jumps, and avoid running. You can stay on an uncracked block of ice for about three seconds. Jump in place and change blocks, just like you would in Hex-A-Gone.

6 DIVE

In the last moments of the round, you will sometimes have to jump and then dive to get over two blocks. You can dive onto a block of ice that's at the point of breaking before moving on to another one. But be careful, you have to be quick . . . and there's no room for error if you want to be the last bean standing.

ACKNOWLEDGMENTS

A big thank you to the entire community of players who constantly share their discoveries for each level. Special thanks to YouTubers KingBlackToof, David1NBA, and Przemobjj, whose explanatory videos you should absolutely watch. Thanks also to Sharky, TT linklarcher, jalayannrush, Gorvi, and all the players who follow me on YouTube and Twitch, and with whom I've shared epic moments in this game.

Come and find me live on YouTube (Stef Leflou) and Twitch (Stef_leflou).